OLD COUNTRY ROAD
SCHOOL LIBRARY

WAYNE GRETZKY

WAYNE GRETZKY

The Great One
by Andrew Santella

A Book Report Biography
FRANKLIN WATTS
A Division of Grolier Publishing
New York / London / Hong Kong / Sydney
Danbury, Connecticut

Cover illustration by James Mellett from photographs by
Sam Mircovich and Associated Press.

Photographs ©: Allsport USA: 99 (Al Bello), 101 (Robert Laberce);
Archive Photos: 90 (Lee); Bruce Bennett Studios: 40, 12, 19, 21, 29, 32,
34, 42, 49, 53, 56, 59, 64, 67, 69, 81, 86, 88, 92 (Bruce Bennett);
Reuters/Corbis-Bettmann: 75, 78, 79, 61; Sportschrome East/West:
97 (Bongarts/ Mark Sandten), 72 (DBS Photography), 15 (Rob
Tringali, Jr.); UPI/Corbis-Bettmann: 2, 37, 46, 55, 70.

Visit Franklin Watts on the Internet at:
http://publishing.grolier.com

Library of Congress Cataloging-in-Publication Data

Santella, Andrew.
    Wayne Gretzky : the great one / by Andrew Santella.
        p. cm.—(a book report biography)
    Includes bibliographical references and index.
    Summary: Describes the personal life and hockey career of one of the
    greatest players in the NHL, Wayne Gretzky.
    ISBN 0-531-11567-4 (lib. bgd.)   0-531-15954-X (pbk.)
    1. Gretzky, Wayne, 1961– —Juvenile literature. 2. Hockey players—
Canada—Biography—Juvenile literature. [1. Gretzky, Wayne, 1961– . 2.
    Hockey players.] I. Title. II. Series.
    GV848.5.G73S36   1999
    796.962'092—dc21
    [B]   98–17976
                                                              CIP
                                                               AC

© 1998 by Franklin Watts, a division of Grolier Publishing
All rights reserved. Published simultaneously in Canada
Printed in the United States of America
1 2 3 4 5 6 7 8 9 10 R 08 07 06 05 04 03 02 01 00 99

GROLIER
PUBLISHING

CONTENTS

CHAPTER ONE
THE HAPPIEST KID IN CANADA
9

CHAPTER TWO
THE WORLD'S SHORTEST CHILDHOOD
17

CHAPTER THREE
TRADED AT AGE SEVENTEEN
28

CHAPTER FOUR
A MILLION MILES FROM THE SOO
36

CHAPTER FIVE
A SEASON FOR THE RECORD BOOKS
45

CHAPTER SIX
THE FIRST CUP
51

CHAPTER SEVEN
GRETZKY AT THE ALTAR
58

CHAPTER EIGHT
L.A. STORY
63

CHAPTER NINE
PASSING GORDIE HOWE
74

CHAPTER TEN
MOVING ON
84

CHAPTER ELEVEN
GRETZKY AND THE GLOBAL GAME
94

CHRONOLOGY
103

A NOTE ON SOURCES
105

FOR FURTHER READING
107

INDEX
109

WAYNE GRETZKY

CHAPTER ONE

THE HAPPIEST KID IN CANADA

Wayne Gretzky first took to the ice in 1963. One November morning, on the frozen Nith River below his grandparents' farm in Ontario, two-year-old Wayne went skating. He did what most first-time skaters do. He wobbled, he flailed his arms, he lost his balance, he fell. Then he got up and tried again, and again, and again.

Wayne's father captured every moment on his movie camera. Anyone who looks at that old film would have a hard time finding hints of the greatness to come. Who could have guessed that the little blond kid with the sawed-off hockey stick would become one of the world's most famous athletes? Who would have believed that the kid buried beneath the cap and scarf and snow pants would break hockey record after hockey record? Who could have known that the little boy picking himself up off the ice would one day be called "The Great Gretzky"?

A LOVE AFFAIR

Wayne Gretzky's love affair with hockey began that day on the Nith River. It would continue for decades through one of the most remarkable careers in the history of sports.

His passion for hockey kept young Wayne on the ice all day long and far into the night. It made him fire slap shot after slap shot at the side of his grandparents' farmhouse—breaking more than a few windows in the process. It kept him in the city park skating until bedtime. And it made Wayne's father create a backyard ice rink, so that his hockey-crazy boy could practice close to home.

Wayne named the backyard ice rink "Wally Coliseum," in honor of his father, Walter Gretzky. Construction on the Wally Coliseum began when Wayne was four years old. That fall, his father cut the grass very short and when the ground froze, he covered it with a thin layer of snow. Then he dragged the lawn sprinkler out to the middle of the yard, turned it on, and left it running all night. The Gretzky house was probably the only one in Brantford, Ontario, with a lawn sprinkler running that winter night. But when morning came, Wayne had a perfect patch of new ice to skate on, and his proud father could watch his son from the warmth of the kitchen.

From then on, Wayne Gretzky spent most of his winters on the ice. He skated in the morning before school. He skated after school until his mother called him for dinner. He ate in his skates and then headed back out to skate until bedtime. On weekends, Wayne's friends gathered for games at Wally Coliseum. But at night, the ice belonged to Wayne and his father. Wayne developed his skating technique by weaving his way through an obstacle course of empty detergent bottles. He practiced his shooting, aiming for targets—and breaking hockey sticks at the rate of one a month.

Years later, Wayne Gretzky could match a trophy or award or career record for every one of those splintered hockey sticks. But the hours young Wayne Gretzky spent on the ice were never about becoming the world's greatest hockey player. They were about having fun, playing the game he loved.

In fact, Wally Coliseum brought together the two things that mattered most to Wayne—his family and hockey. Most of Wayne's early memories revolve around those two constants in his life.

Wayne's father had played Junior B hockey in Canada. When Wayne was four, he was stickboy for his father's team. Later, Wayne said that his father was his first hero. He also remembered the

Walter Gretzky was a great role model for his son.

many hours his mother spent driving him to distant arenas, waiting through long practices, and then driving him home again. He remembered the whole family watching "Hockey Night in Canada," and he remembered his grandmother playing goalie against him when he was very young.

Wayne Gretzky was born on January 26, 1961, in Brantford, Canada, a city in southern Ontario, near Hamilton. He was the eldest of five children. His father, Walter, was the son of immigrants who ran a vegetable farm outside Brantford. Wayne's grandmother, Mary, came to Canada from Poland when she was twenty-six; his grandfather, Tony, came from Russia. They were hard workers. Following his grandfather around the farm for morning chores, young Wayne must have absorbed some of that work ethic.

When Wayne was twelve-years-old, his grandfather died. In his autobiography, Wayne wrote, "that was the hardest day of my life until the day my grandmother herself died." Wayne's mother and his sister, Kim, took care of his grandmother during her long illness, and his father tended to the farm. It was another lesson in responsibility for the boy.

"That was the hardest day of my life until the day my grandmother herself died."

In Brantford, Wayne's life revolved around the family house on Varadi Avenue. It had just three bedrooms for a family with five children. Wayne's sister, Kim, had a room of her own. His youngest brother, Brent, was born when Wayne was 12 and stayed in his parents' room. That left one eight-foot by six-foot room for Wayne and his brothers Keith and Glen. But that house had one unusual advantage—the backyard ice rink. No wonder Wayne spent so much time on the spacious ice of Wally Coliseum.

With all that ice time, Wayne developed his hockey skills unusually early. By the time he was six, he was a hockey player with nowhere to play. Sure, he still played in pickup games with the bigger kids, but he needed an organized league where he could develop his skills. Unfortunately, Brantford's hockey leagues did not accept players under ten. But finally, six-year-old Wayne got a tryout in the Brantford Atom League. He impressed the coaches enough to win a spot playing with ten-year-olds on the Brantford Nadrofsky novice team.

Wayne was small even for a six-year-old, so his hockey sweater fit him like a tent. To keep it from catching on his stick, his father tucked Wayne's sweater into his pants on the shooting side. It's how Gretzky would wear his uniform for the rest of his playing days.

Even today, Gretzky plays with one side of his jersey tucked in and the other side hanging out.

Wayne scored just one goal that first year, but he was in six-year-old heaven anyway. He was happy to be wearing an official team hockey sweater (number 11), and he enjoyed playing with the big kids. The pressure that comes with being very talented was still in the future. For now,

Wayne Gretzky was having a ball doing what he loved—playing hockey.

"Until I was about twelve. That's when I realized I was the unhappiest."

"I always felt like I was the happiest kid in Canada," Wayne wrote in his autobiography. "Until I was about twelve. That's when I realized I was the unhappiest."

CHAPTER TWO

THE WORLD'S SHORTEST CHILDHOOD

At the end of Wayne's first year of novice hockey, he went to the team's awards banquet with his father. He watched player after player get up to accept a trophy, but there was no trophy for the smallest boy in the room. On the way home, Wayne started crying. "Everybody won a trophy but me," he told his father. "Wayne," Walter replied,

> **"Everybody won a trophy but me."**

"keep practicing and one day you're gonna have so many trophies, we're not gonna have room for them all."

Walter Gretzky's answer proved to be right on the mark. But no one could have predicted the trouble all those trophies would cause Wayne Gretzky. Wayne was still the smallest and the youngest player on his team, but his scoring totals were growing fast. In his second year playing for Brantford Nadrofsky, he scored 27 goals; in his third year, he scored 104; and in his fourth year, his total ballooned to 196.

Then came the breakthrough. In 1971–72, he scored 378 goals in 69 games. These were unheard-of numbers. Wayne won the scoring race by 238 goals. He demolished every other scoring record for that age group and his remarkable performance that season made him a celebrity throughout Canada. He was just ten years old when that season started and he stood four feet four inches tall. But ready or not, Wayne Gretzky was in the public eye—to stay.

THE GREAT GRETZKY

In a story about Wayne, a sportswriter from London, Ontario, called him "The Great Gretzky." The name stuck, though it always made Wayne feel a little uncomfortable. Friends at school started asking for his autograph and he did countless interviews with reporters. When his team traveled to out-of-town tournaments, they found signs advertising their arrival: "See Wayne Gretzky—Ten-Year-Old Scoring Ace."

For the ten-year-old scoring ace, the season was "a dream and a nightmare at the same time."

Although a young player, Wayne attracted enormous attention due to his incredible talent.

Gretzky remembers that "it was the first time unhappiness had crept into my life." All the attention was hard for the quiet ten-year-old to take, and, worse yet, his stardom bred envy and resentment in the parents of his teammates. They began accusing him of hogging the puck. They booed him during introductions. They made it hard for his parents to even watch Wayne play.

"It was the first time unhappiness had crept into my life."

Adoration and applause one moment and jealousy and backbiting the next were enough to confuse and hurt anybody, especially a boy still in grade school. Later, Wayne would say that he'd had "the world's shortest childhood."

Not surprisingly, Wayne started trying to hide from the attention. He often sent his best friend and teammate Greg Stefan out to sign autographs for him, wearing a team jacket with Wayne's name on it. Unfortunately, Stefan often spelled Wayne's name "Gretsky."

In any case, there was no hiding from the fact that Wayne Gretzky was an extraordinarily gifted hockey player. His talents, in fact, were making it difficult for him to live anything close to a normal life. For a while, Wayne also played lacrosse and

Wayne holds one of the first of many trophies he would earn through his storied career.

baseball, but soon he had to give up everything except hockey. In later years, Wayne had regrets about his inability to pursue other interests. "I liked baseball so much, but I couldn't throw hockey away," he said. "If I could have, I would have done both."

"I liked baseball so much, but I couldn't throw hockey away,"

It was becoming clear that Wayne would have to give up much more than baseball. It wasn't long before the young phenom had outgrown Brantford. He traveled around Canada and met people he'd always dreamed of meeting. When he was eleven, he got tips from his hockey idol, Gordie Howe. Howe was immediately won over by Gretzky. "I liked Wayne right away," he said. "He said Mr. and Mrs. a lot. He said please and thank you." At thirteen, Montreal Canadian great Jean Beliveau came to see him play. But the more acclaim Wayne got, the more difficult his life in Brantford became.

JUNIOR B HOCKEY

Finally, a solution to Wayne's problems appeared. When Wayne was fourteen, he was given the opportunity to move to Toronto, play Junior B hockey, and live with the family of a teammate. It would give him the chance to develop his hockey skills at a higher level and also to escape the jealousy swirling around him in Brantford. But it would mean moving away from his family, away from the people who had supported him through good times and bad.

But first, Wayne had to convince his parents that he was ready for the move. They were naturally reluctant to let their teenage son move to the big city. But eventually they relented and Wayne Gretzky left home. He was only fourteen years old, he weighed 135 pounds, and he was playing against twenty-one-year olds. But he immediately ended any doubts about his right to play in Toronto by scoring two goals in his first game.

In Toronto, for the first time in years, Wayne could play hockey without being booed or worrying about the nasty comments his parents overheard in the stands. And he could go to school like anyone else and not have people ask him for his autograph. But he still had to learn to live away from home. Though there were frequent phone calls and weekend trips home, there was also a lot of sadness and loneliness. It was hard to feel like part of the same close-knit family he'd always known. His youngest brother, Brent, was growing up while Wayne had to move away. "To him, for quite a while, I'm afraid I wasn't so much a big brother as a hockey superstar who spent the night now and again," Wayne remembered.

> "To him, for quite a while, I'm afraid I wasn't so much a big brother as a hockey superstar who spent the night now and again."

But Wayne's abilities had placed him on the fast track and there was no turning back. He was ready to make the jump to professional hockey. He was just a scrawny sixteen-year-old when the Sault Ste. Marie Greyhounds used their first draft pick to select Wayne Gretzky.

THE SOO

Sault Ste. Marie is a town of about 32,000 in southern Ontario, across from the Upper Peninsula of Michigan. Locals call it "the Soo." Wayne and his father had hoped he wouldn't be drafted by the Greyhounds. When he was chosen, they flew to the Soo to tell the general manager, Angelo Bumbacco, that Wayne would not play there. But Bumbacco won them over.

The Greyhounds arranged for Wayne to live with a family the Gretzkys knew from Pee Wee hockey and Coach Muzz MacPherson promised that Wayne would play a lot. Then Bumbacco said that if Wayne was injured or cut from the Greyhounds, the team would pay for his college education. That promise convinced Wayne's family.

The Greyhounds play in the Ontario Hockey Association (OHA), a Junior A league. While it is professional hockey, it's not exactly big time. Wayne's salary was only $25 a week, but Wayne wasn't worried about the money. He was, after all, still in high school, and he hardly had time to spend money anyway. Wayne's life in the Soo was a blur of classes, homework, practice, and grueling road trips. It was not unusual for the team to return home from an away game at three in the morning. That left Wayne just enough time for a short nap before school started.

Young as he was, Wayne was living in a grown-up world. Junior A hockey is rough and sometimes dirty. For many players, Junior A is their last chance at a hockey career, and they will do whatever it takes to make it to the next level. Coach MacPherson demanded a lot from his team. When the Greyhounds played a lackluster game on the road one night, MacPherson brought the team back to their arena and made them practice in the middle of the night in their street clothes.

As he did wherever he played, Wayne stood out in the Soo. For one thing, he started wearing number 99. He'd always wanted to wear number

9, the number worn by Gordie Howe, but that number was taken by another player. So Wayne tried 99. Traditionally, hockey players wore numbers lower than 35. At the time Wayne switched, only a few NHL stars were wearing high numbers like Phil Esposito's 77 or Ken Hodge's 88. For a player still working his way up through Junior hockey, breaking hockey tradition struck some fans as cocky. But Wayne pulled it off. The first night he wore 99, he scored three goals. Knowing a lucky number when he saw one, Wayne never wore another number.

Above all, Wayne stood out by his performance on the ice. He scored 70 goals and 182 points in 64 games—a point total that shattered the 'all-time Junior A scoring record. It's still the record for most points ever scored by a rookie. To no one's surprise, Wayne's remarkable performance made him the OHA's 1977–78 Rookie of the Year.

When Coach MacPherson decided to leave the Greyhounds, Wayne figured it might be time for him to try the next level. Word was out about the sensational young player tearing up the OHA in the Soo. General managers in the National Hockey League were watching Wayne's progress closely. And Wayne felt sure he was ready for big-time professional hockey. But the NHL did not allow players under the age of 18. That left the rene-gade World Hockey Association (WHA).

The WHA had a colorful history, but it lasted just seven years. Its teams always seemed to be on the verge of bankruptcy and attendance was sparse. Franchise moves were frequent, and—to the horror of hockey traditionalists—the pucks were orange. But the WHA had some outstanding hockey players—all-time greats like Bobby Hull and Gordie Howe. And, of course, it was the WHA that gave Wayne Gretzky his shot at the big time.

CHAPTER THREE

TRADED AT AGE SEVENTEEN

In the summer of 1977, Wayne Gretzky earned $5 an hour patching potholes. One year later, in June 1978, he signed an $825,000 contract to play hockey for the Indianapolis Racers of the WHA. It was a significant raise.

Actually, Wayne's contract wasn't with the Racers but with their owner, Nelson Skalbania. The two drew up the final terms on Skalbania's private plane, and the twelfth-grader wrote the contract himself, using school notebook paper to keep the lines straight. It was an unusual arrangement, a "personal services" contract. Skalbania joked that if hockey didn't work out for Gretzky, he could still find work on Skalbania's yacht. Needless to say, Wayne never became a deckhand.

But neither did he take Indianapolis by storm. Years later, when Wayne went to Los Ange-

Even Wayne Gretzky couldn't make the Indianapolis Racers a popular team.

les to play for the NHL's Kings, much would be made of how he popularized hockey in the United States. But not even Wayne Gretzky could turn Indianapolis on to professional hockey in 1978. For the kid from hockey-mad Canada, Indianapolis was a rude awakening. This was a city with no hockey tradition at all. Winter in Indiana meant basketball.

The team sent Gretzky out on personal appearances at malls to sign autographs, sell tickets, and drum up interest in the Racers. But there was very little response. Crowds did not exactly mob Gretzky for his autograph. It was quite a change from Brantford, where his celebrity had caused him so much trouble.

In Gretzky's second game for the Racers, he ran up against Gordie Howe's New England Whalers. When seven-year-old Wayne got a Gordie Howe hockey sweater for Christmas, he wore it everywhere he went. Now Gretzky was playing professional hockey against his idol, one of the most respected and toughest players in the history of the game. During one game, Gretzky made the mistake of stealing the puck from Howe. That earned him a painful crack across the thumb from Howe's stick and a lesson in hockey etiquette: don't show up the legend, especially when he's as tough as Gordie Howe.

In his eight games with the Racers, Gretzky had three goals and three assists. Attendance was unimpressive. The team drew a respectable 11,000 people for their opener, but fewer than 6,000 per game from then on. Gretzky fever was not exactly sweeping Indianapolis.

Meanwhile, Skalbania was losing money on the Racers. The only solution seemed to be trading the young phenom in hopes of reviving the team's fortunes. So, at seventeen, Wayne Gretzky found himself headed for Edmonton to join his new team, the Oilers. And it turned out to be the start of something big—for Edmonton as well as for Gretzky.

GRETZKY AND THE EDMONTON OILERS

Edmonton was ready for Wayne Gretzky. It was a hockey-crazy town, for one thing. The year before Gretzky arrived, the Oilers led the WHA in attendance. The town was in the middle of an oil boom, times were good, and rumors had it that the Oilers might soon be asked to join the NHL.

Even the Oilers' coach, Glen Sather, laid out the red carpet for Wayne Gretzky. The first time Sather saw him practice, he thought Gretzky was one of the players' kids. After all, Gretzky was still only seventeen. At their first meeting, Sather told

Gretzky poses in an Edmonton Oiler uniform.

Gretzky he'd put him up until Gretzky found a place of his own. He also told him that he expected big things of Gretzky.

"One day, we're gonna be in the NHL and one day you're going to be captain of this hockey team," Sather told the new arrival. Gretzky was dumbstruck. He was the youngest guy on the team, by three years. He was worried about just fitting in and here was the coach telling him that he would one day lead the team.

> "One day, we're gonna be in the NHL and one day you're going to be captain of this hockey team."

Sather wasn't the only one who showed confidence in Gretzky. The Oilers' owner, Peter Pocklington, signed him to a contract without ever having seen him play. Gretzky signed that contract on his eighteenth birthday. Pocklington had ordered an enormous cake for the occasion, shaped like the number 99, and brought it out to center ice. Gretzky's new contract, served up alongside the cake, offered him $3 million for ten years. Gretzky signed the contract, but he never got the cake. One of his teammates sat on it.

The Oilers made it to the WHA finals that year, before losing to the Winnipeg Jets. Nobody knew it at the time, but it would be the last

Gretzky stands in the locker room after the last game to be played in the WHA.

WHA championship series. Gretzky had done much to prove himself, scoring 43 goals, collecting 104 points, and earning Rookie of the Year honors in the league. But not everyone was a believer. Some people said he was too slow to star in the NHL, others said he was too small. As it turned out, he would soon have the chance to prove them all wrong.

CHAPTER FOUR

A MILLION MILES FROM THE SOO

While the WHA was on its last legs, the NHL had its eyes on a few of its strongest teams, including Edmonton. In 1979, the NHL absorbed four WHA teams—the Quebec Nordiques, Winnipeg Jets, Hartford Whalers, and the Edmonton Oilers. At eighteen, Wayne Gretzky had arrived at hockey's highest level.

LIFE IN THE NHL

Gretzky's first NHL season was a real test. Like any newcomer to the league, he had to learn to live with its grueling 80-game schedule and numbingly long road trips. To make matters worse, Gretzky was hampered most of the season by tonsillitis. He ran a fever, nursed a sore throat, and at times was unable to speak.

The good news was that Gretzky was joined in Edmonton by a pair of remarkable young hockey players—defenseman Kevin Lowe and center Mark Messier. Gretzky and Messier were eighteen; Lowe was nineteen. The three would form

Gretzky jokes with an Edmonton teammate during warm-ups.

the nucleus of the great Oiler teams of the near future and become best friends in the process. Gretzky and Lowe even agreed to share an apartment, so Gretzky finally moved out of the coach's house. The three up-and-coming stars learned the ropes together in Edmonton. Veterans, such as Ace Bailey, taught them the ins and outs of life in the big leagues. Lowe practiced his cooking skills on roommate Gretzky. Like most kids who grow up playing hockey, they'd dreamed of playing in the NHL and now they were seeing their dreams come true. Gretzky recalled sitting in a hotel room with Messier on the eve of the Oilers' first road game and soaking up the glorious feeling. They were in the NHL!

One aspect of NHL life, though, bothered Gretzky. He was afraid of flying. Take-offs and landings left him drenched in sweat. Hypnosis and a host of other cures eventually reduced his fear. But in any case, it never stopped Gretzky from achieving on the ice. He was driven by the critics who doubted his ability to thrive in the NHL. He'd proved the doubters wrong at every other level, dating back to Pee Wee hockey, and he was determined to do the same in the NHL. He vowed to contend for the league's scoring title. It was a lofty goal, and even his father, Gretzky's biggest supporter, had his doubts.

That year, Gretzky didn't score his first goal until the fifth game. But by the All-Star break, he was on fire. He had seven points in one game, coming within one point of breaking the record. His early season performance was enough to win him second-team NHL All-Star honors, but he really turned it on during the second half of the season.

Gretzky piled up the goals and assists, and with 18 games left to play, he was within 20 points of the league leaders, the great Marcel Dionne and Guy Lafleur. On April 2, he scored his 50th goal. At nineteen, he was the youngest player in the history of the NHL to reach that milestone.

In a game at Toronto, his two goals and four assists tied him with Dionne for the league lead. The two were still tied at the end of the season, but the scoring title went to Dionne because he had more goals. Gretzky was also denied the Rookie of the Year award, when the league ruled that his year in the WHA disqualified him.

He did win the Lady Byng Trophy, which honors sportsmanship. Many hockey players scoff at this award, but Gretzky prized it as a recognition of the way he played the game. And greater recognition was still to come. Gretzky won the coveted Hart Trophy as the league's Most Valuable Player. It was an astounding feat—no first-year player had ever won that award.

*Gretzky is congratulated after scoring one of the
many goals he would tally up during
his rookie season.*

The MVP trophy rewarded Gretzky's extraor-
dinary second-half performance, which propelled
his team into the playoffs. Behind Gretzky, the
Oilers won or tied their last nine games to clinch
the final playoff spot. In the 1980 playoffs, the Oilers were swept by the Philadelphia Flyers, the
NHL's top team. But the brief playoff experience

left the young team hungry for more. The Flyers' leader, Bobby Clarke, was impressed with the Oilers' gritty showing and said they would be a team to reckon with in the future. Gretzky agreed—and he knew that the future was right around the corner.

In the off-season, the Oilers added more talent, picking up Paul Coffey, Jari Kurri, Glenn Anderson, and Andy Moog in the draft. Each of these players had a big part in the emerging Oiler dynasty. Playing alongside talented scorers like Kurri and Anderson, Gretzky's amazing playmaking skills blossomed. In 1980–81, he broke Bobby Orr's single-season assist record and Phil Esposito's single-season point total. And once more, Gretzky caught fire in the home stretch, finishing with 164 points, including 34 goals in his last 40 games. The Oilers made the playoffs again.

MIRACLE IN MONTREAL

Their first-round opponent was the Montreal Canadiens, the league's most famous franchise. They'd won four straight Stanley Cups in the 1970s, and their home, the Montreal Forum, was a shrine to hockey fans. The Canadiens were considered all but unbeatable at home. The upstart Oilers from Edmonton, the team left over from the WHA, entered the historic Forum in awe. So

Gretzky shoots and scores!

many great teams and great players had occupied the visitors' dressing room at the Forum—and so many had gone home losers. But the upstart Oilers would not be disappointed. They took two straight games from the shocked home team. Gretzky had five assists in the first game, a playoff record. The Oilers won the second game 3–1, and even the classy Montreal fans applauded their amazing performance.

Back in Edmonton, the Oilers won the third game 6–2, behind Gretzky's three goals and an assist, to take the series. Some people called it the biggest upset in Stanley Cup history—the "Miracle in Montreal."

The Oilers celebrated like the kids they were. They splashed in the locker-room whirlpool. All through the series, the team had chanted on the bench, "Here we go Oilers, here we go . . ." It may have been amateurish, but it worked. "I know it's high-schoolish, but we're all barely out of high school," Gretzky explained. "We're the youngest team in the NHL, just a bunch of kids with nothing to lose."

"We're the youngest team in the NHL, just a bunch of kids with nothing to lose."

The Miracle in Montreal earned the Oilers the right to face an even more fearsome opponent, the Stanley Cup–champion New York Islanders. Gretzky later admitted that the Oilers were "petrified" to be playing the Islanders. After all, the Oilers featured six players young enough to still be playing Junior hockey.

The Oilers lost that series four games to two. But the team had made great strides in that pivotal season—and so had Gretzky. He'd led his team to a monumental upset over the Montreal Canadiens, and he'd won his second straight Hart Trophy as the NHL's Most Valuable Player. He called it an "unforgettable season."

"Everything I'd ever wanted was coming true."

"Everything I'd ever wanted was coming true," Gretzky later wrote, "I was playing big-time NHL hockey with a team that was improving all the time, and I was proving I could stay with anybody. The Soo seemed a million miles away."

CHAPTER FIVE

A SEASON FOR THE RECORD BOOKS

Wayne Gretzky's 1981–82 season changed the hockey world's notions about what a single player could achieve. He scored 92 goals. Nobody had ever done that. He scored his first 50 goals in just 39 games. Nobody had ever done that either. He registered 212 points. And, for sure, nobody had ever done that.

In fact, nobody had even come close to these numbers. In 1981–82, Wayne Gretzky didn't just break records, he demolished them. For example, his 92 goals were 16 more than the previous record. If some baseball player of the future were to exceed Roger Maris's record of 61 home runs in a season by the same percentage, he'd finish with 73 home runs. That kind of performance would turn the world of baseball on its head, and that's just what Gretzky's showing in 1981–82 did for hockey. At season's end, he had accumulated a tro-

Gretzky (left) is surrounded by teammates after breaking the record for goals scored in a season.

phy case full of NHL single-season records: points, goals, assists (120) and hat tricks (10). What's more, he'd led the Oilers to the NHL's best record.

Gretzky began that season with a bad taste in his mouth from the 1981 Canada Cup series, the international hockey tournament that matched up the world's best national teams. Gretzky played poorly and his Canadian team was crushed by the Russian team 8–1 in the final. The loss was a blow to Canadian national pride, and with some fans blaming him for the loss, Gretzky felt as if he'd let his country down. He determined to become more aggressive in the coming season.

Sure enough, Gretzky began passing less and shooting more, and the goals piled up. He scored 13 times in his first 13 games, then 4 in the next game against Quebec. He kept up that pace and then surged with 10 goals in 4 games in late December. In one magical game in Edmonton against the Philadelphia Flyers, he broke loose with 5 goals, giving him 50 goals in just 39 games. Nobody in the NHL had ever scored 50 times in fewer than 50 games. Gretzky did it with 10 games to spare.

The speed with which Gretzky reached the 50-goal mark surprised even his father. "After the game, I went into the locker room and I called my dad and I think it was the first time I might have shocked my father, in that I had done something unique," Gretzky recalled. "The timing for me was perfect. I played with the right team and with the right players."

The next record to fall was Phil Esposito's single-season mark of 76. Gretzky broke that record in Buffalo, with his father in attendance. His mother would have been there, too, but she was back in Canada watching Wayne's younger brother Brent play in a Pee Wee tournament. As his mother likes to remind people, there is more than one hockey player in the Gretzky family.

Gretzky passed the 200-point mark—where no hockey player had ever gone—in Calgary. Calgary fans loved to boo Gretzky and the archrival Oilers. "I've been booed before, but here they boo me like they really mean it," Gretzky commented. Sure enough, Calgary fans started the night booing Gretzky. But by the time Wayne made hockey history with four more points, they were giving him standing ovations. This time, both Mr. and Mrs. Gretzky were in attendance.

PLAYOFF PROBLEMS

It was a glorious season for Gretzky and the Oilers. The team was winning big, earning the top spot in the playoff pairings. Gretzky seemed to be breaking another record every night and astounding his teammates in the process. But the dream season turned nightmarish in the playoffs. The Oilers were ambushed in the first round by the Los Angeles Kings. The Oilers blew early leads in two games and let the Kings skate away with the series. Gretzky's miracle season was over.

The loss was hard to swallow, but it was another step in the growing process for the young team. They came back the next year determined to get a shot at the Stanley Cup. This time, they avoided the first-round upset. In fact, they roared through the 1983 playoffs, crushing Winnipeg, Calgary, and Chicago to make it to the Stanley Cup finals. Then they ran into the three-time defending champion New York Islanders. It was no contest. The Oilers were determined, but the champion Islanders were not about to surrender the Cup to the upstarts from out west. Not yet, anyway. They swept the Oilers four games to none.

After Game Three of the series, Gretzky's father criticized him for his lackluster effort in

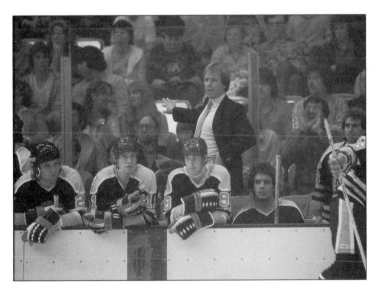

Gretzky and the Oilers were still too inexperienced to win the Stanley Cup in 1983.

one practice. Later, when Gretzky was back home during the off-season, his father pointed out Gretzky's grandmother, then 79 years old, toiling in the garden. He reminded the superstar that with the Stanley Cup on the line, he had given less than a maximum effort. It was a lesson that would stick with Gretzky.

CHAPTER SIX

THE FIRST CUP

Wayne Gretzky had won four straight Hart Trophies as the NHL's Most Valuable Player. *Sports Illustrated* had named him their Sportsman of the Year. He'd won countless trophies and broken so many records it was hard to keep track. But one prize still eluded him—the Stanley Cup.

It was something his critics never failed to point out. Gretzky knew he would never be considered a truly great player, an all-time great, until he helped the Oilers win a Stanley Cup. There is probably no trophy in sports as treasured as the Stanley Cup—the goal of every NHL player. But winning the Cup was more than a goal for Gretzky—it was a mission. The players he admired most, players like Gordie Howe, had always come through in big games and had all won Stanley Cups. Gretzky wanted to be remembered that way.

"So many times as a kid watching 'Hockey Night in Canada,' you see Jean Beliveau lifting the Stanley Cup and Bobby Orr lifting the Stanley Cup," Gretzky recalled. "One day you want to be the guy able to lift that thing."

CAPTAIN GRETZKY

At the same time, Gretzky was emerging as a leader of the Oilers. Their captain, Lee Fogolin, recognized this and insisted that Gretzky take over as captain for the 1983–84 season. Hockey tradition requires that the captain of each team wear the letter C on his sweater. It's an honor and a responsibility. By handing Gretzky the C, Fogolin was telling the young superstar that he was ready to lead the Oilers to the Stanley Cup. He was also fulfilling Sather's prophecy of years earlier.

It was a vote of confidence in Gretzky and the other young stars, and Gretzky responded. He started the season on a tear. Despite an aching shoulder, he scored in each of his first 51 games. It was by far the longest streak of consecutive scoring games in NHL history. It gave Gretzky another NHL record.

But his eyes were on a team goal. That season, he received plenty of help. Teammates Glenn Anderson and Jari Kurri had remarkable seasons, scoring 54 and 52 goals respectively. No NHL

*In recognition of his outstanding play, Gretzky
became captain of the Oilers at the start
of the 1983–84 season.*

team had ever had three 50-goal scorers. Still, despite all that talent, the team had stumbled in the playoffs the last two seasons. In 1984, though, the Oilers played like a much more mature team. And Gretzky was virtually unstoppable in the playoffs, racking up 35 points in 19 games.

The Oilers swept Winnipeg, defeated their rivals from Calgary, then swept Minnesota. Waiting for them in the Stanley Cup finals, of course, were the feared New York Islanders. The Islanders shut down Gretzky in the first two games, at Long Island, but the Oilers still managed to win one. Back in Edmonton, Gretzky and the Oilers finally broke through. Gretzky had two goals each in Games Four and Five. It was part of a 19–6 scoring barrage in the last three games that let the Oilers bury their main rival. Edmonton won the series three games to one and captured the Stanley Cup.

Gretzky would later rank that first Cup as the greatest of his accomplishments in hockey. It put to rest years of frustration and near misses for the Oilers. And it silenced, once and for all, the critics who said that Gretzky could not win the big one.

Winning the Cup at home made it even sweeter. After the trophy presentation, Gretzky, wearing the captain's C on his sweater, skated the Cup around the rink, displaying it to the fans who had watched him come of age in Edmonton.

Gretzky joyfully raises the Stanley Cup over his head after defeating the New York Islanders.

"I remember the last few seconds of the game, just thinking, 'I've waited my whole life for this. This is going to be the most enjoyable moment of my life,'" Gretzky recalled. And those five seconds summed up a life of commitment and hard work, not only for me, but for every player on

Gretzky holds his younger brother Brent while giving an interview after winning the Stanley Cup.

our hockey team to finally get a chance to lift the Stanley Cup."

After he had skated his victory lap with the Cup, Gretzky took another trip around the rink, this time carrying his little brother Brent on his shoulders.

CHAPTER SEVEN

GRETZKY AT THE ALTAR

To this day, Wayne Gretzky says that his greatest game might not have been a hockey game. More than his many spectacular moments on the ice, he remembers the Boston Celtics–Los Angeles Lakers basketball game he attended in 1987. It was there that he met his future wife, actress Janet Jones.

Actually, Jones and Gretzky had met several times before, without really getting to know each other. But when they were reintroduced at that basketball game, the two suddenly hit it off. After the game, they went to dinner with friends and had such a good time that they decided to see each other again. They discovered that they had much in common. Like Gretzky, Jones was something of a child prodigy, and her budding career as a dancer and actress kept her from having much of a normal childhood. Both were caught up in the obligations and commitments and constant travel

In 1987, Gretzky found a loving companion in actress Janet Jones.

that come with being a celebrity, but deep down they longed for a traditional family life.

Their romance went public when Jones accompanied Gretzky to the 1987 Canada Cup training camp. Gretzky took some criticism for the relationship. Canadian fans, protective of their home-grown star, wanted to know why he had to date an American woman. Plus, there were adjustments to make. Before she met Gretzky, Jones had never seen a hockey game in her life. After her first game, she thought Gretzky might have injured himself, because he kept coming off the ice after skating a minute at a time. He had to explain to her that hockey players always skate in brief shifts.

Before they were married in Edmonton on July 16, 1988, plans for the marriage were front-page news for weeks. Newspapers reported on everything from the guest list to the cost of the bride's dress. They called it "Canada's Royal Wedding." The media attention was so overwhelming that the couple briefly considered eloping, but the wedding took place as scheduled. It was covered live on national television. Seven hundred guests attended, and 10,000 fans stood outside the church waiting for a glimpse of the couple. Gretzky said later that he was more nervous during the ceremony than during any hockey game he'd ever played in.

*Gretzky and Janet Jones smile after
finishing their vows.*

The newlyweds settled into their new home in Edmonton, ready to start their new life together. Jones even resigned herself to putting her career on hold: Edmonton, after all, is a long, long way from Hollywood. But, as it turned out, a big move was already in the works—one that would change their lives forever.

CHAPTER EIGHT

L.A. STORY

Meanwhile, Gretzky and the Oilers rolled on. They won their second consecutive Stanley Cup in 1985. In 1986, Gretzky broke his own single-season scoring record by tallying 215 points. After faltering in the playoffs that year, the Oilers came back to win consecutive Stanley Cups in 1987 and 1988. Gretzky earned his eighth consecutive Hart Trophy as the NHL's Most Valuable Player, an astounding total. The 1988 Stanley Cup was Edmonton's fourth in five years. The average age of the players on that team was 25. It looked like the Oilers would go on collecting Cups for years to come. After beating the Boston Bruins for that fourth title, Gretzky gathered his teammates together for a group picture at center ice. Nobody knew it at the time, but it was the last time that remarkable group would be together as the Edmonton Oilers.

Gretzky and Mark Messier embrace after winning the Stanley Cup in 1985.

As for Gretzky, he was playing his best hockey yet. The 1987 Canada Cup may well have been the zenith of Gretzky's hockey career. Playing with and against the world's best, he scored 21 goals in 9 games to lead Canada to the championship over the Soviet Union. Gretzky had always been proud to represent Canada in international competition, but the 1987 series was something special for him. He said it was the best performance of his career and few would disagree. It established him without doubt as the best player in the world. It was also a perfect example of how Gretzky elevated the play of those around him. In 1987, he inspired the talented Mario Lemieux of the Pittsburgh Penguins to play his best, too. Lemieux scored the decisive goal on a pass from Gretzky.

But even with the Stanley Cups and personal achievements, Gretzky's Edmonton Oilers were struggling financially. Their owner, Peter Pocklington, needed to raise cash to keep the team afloat, and one of his most valuable assets was Wayne Gretzky. While the Oilers were on their way to winning their fourth championship in five years, Pocklington began discussions with other teams about trading hockey's biggest superstar.

Finally, on August 9, 1988, the Oilers and the Los Angeles Kings announced one of the biggest blockbuster trades in the history of professional sports. The Oilers sent Gretzky and teammates Marty McSorley and Mike Krushelnyski to Los Angeles for Jimmy Carson, Martin Gelinas, three first-round draft picks, and $15 million.

The negotiations leading up to the trade left Gretzky emotionally torn. On the one hand, he was not ready to leave Edmonton. It was there he'd come of age and it was there he'd helped turn an upstart team from the WHA into one of the NHL's greatest dynasties. He had friends in

Edmonton and was even preparing to start a family there. He and Janet Jones had begun searching for a new house.

On the other hand, it seemed like the time might be right for a change. As early as 1987, Gretzky had considered quitting hockey altogether. He was exhausted. At an age when many people are just getting serious about their careers, Gretzky had already played ten years at hockey's highest level. All those extra playoff games and Canada Cup games had taken their toll physically. And the pressure of being Canada's biggest celebrity and its national sport's greatest player was wearing him down emotionally.

In addition, there were problems with Coach Glen Sather. Though Gretzky always appreciated Sather's confidence in him when he was still a skinny, unproven rookie, the coach's demanding style increasingly grated on Gretzky. And Gretzky believed that Pocklington, the Oilers' owner, wasn't treating him fairly either. So when news of the trade negotiations got back to Gretzky, he was willing to consider the possibility of moving on. As the game's biggest star, Gretzky had much more say about his future than most players would. But he felt that if the Oilers were willing to trade him, he might as well be willing to leave.

But even Gretzky couldn't have been prepared for the public's reaction to the trade.

Gretzky, cast in bronze, raises the Stanley Cup in triumph outside Edmonton's arena.

Edmonton fans felt stunned and betrayed. Indeed, hockey fans all over Canada mourned the trade as if they'd been robbed of a national treasure. Some fans even accused Janet Jones of engineering the trade so that she could return to Hollywood and her career. The criticism stung both Jones and Gretzky. But most of all, Edmonton fans knew that they were losing hockey's greatest star. Not long after the trade, the city erected a six-foot bronze statue of Gretzky hoisting the Stanley Cup in front of the Oilers' arena. It was a remarkable honor for a player who was still active.

The press conference announcing the trade was covered live on national television in Canada. When Gretzky tried to explain how much he would miss Edmonton, his emotions overcame him. He began crying. Most Edmonton fans probably felt like crying, too. For ten years, they'd watched Gretzky develop into an all-time great, and they'd seen their team climb to the top of the NHL. Now they were losing him.

BRIGHT LIGHTS, BIG CITY

Arriving in Los Angeles, Gretzky was in the spotlight again. Reporters filled the room to overflowing at his first press conference as a Los Angeles King. Bruce McNall, the Kings' owner, was hoping Gretzky could turn Los Angeles onto hockey.

Unable to contain his emotions, Gretzky tearfully addresses the press before leaving Edmonton.

Judging by the intense interest in the trade, it looked like southern Californians were swept up in some kind of hockey fever.

Gretzky was interviewed on hundreds of television and radio stations and in newspapers. That summer, he hosted hockey clinics and appeared at speaking engagements to promote hockey and the

In Los Angeles, Gretzky and Kings owner
Bruce McNall hold up Gretzky's new uniform.

Los Angeles Kings. Since their founding in 1967, the Kings had always managed to just get by. They were always overshadowed by the more popular Lakers and Dodgers. But with Gretzky on the scene, the Kings' fortunes revived. Season-ticket sales tripled in just two years. Attendance shot up from an average of about 12,000 people per game to about 15,000. Movie stars like Sylvester Stallone and Kevin Costner suddenly started showing up in the Kings' locker room. Games that used to draw 8,000 fans to the arena, were now attracting crowds of 16,000, and within a few years, the Kings were selling out every home game. Not even the Lakers had been able to do that. Soon, everywhere you looked in southern California, fans were wearing Kings jerseys and Kings caps.

Gretzky's influence was felt beyond Los Angeles too. The National Hockey League wanted to put more teams in more warm-weather American cities, where interest in hockey had traditionally been low. Having the game's greatest superstar in one of America's biggest cities—and a media capital—raised hockey's visibility in the United States. And the Kings' success assured the NHL that it could be successful in the South and West. In 1991, the league added a team in San Jose, California, and in 1993, it added another in Anaheim. It wouldn't be long before NHL franchises were springing up in Tampa, Miami, Dallas, and even Phoenix. Most of the credit for hockey's newfound popularity in the United States rested squarely on the shoulders of Wayne Gretzky.

But for all the attention being lavished on the superstar in his glamorous new hometown, Gretzky still had his work cut out for him. This was, after all, a huge challenge. The Kings had paid an

*As captain of the Kings, Gretzky was once
again cast into the limelight.*

enormous amount of money for his services and he knew he would have to prove his worth all over again. A lot of people would be watching to see if he would fall on his face in the bright lights of Los Angeles—most of all, the fans of the Edmonton Oilers. Wayne Gretzky was in a new city, but he was back where he'd been so many times before— under pressure. "The one thing I worried about," he confessed, "was being a $15-million bust."

CHAPTER NINE

PASSING GORDIE HOWE

Los Angeles hockey fans didn't have to wait long for Gretzky to make an impact on his new team. On his first shot in the first game of the season, he scored a goal. The Kings won their first four games, their best start ever. Behind Gretzky, they unleashed an amazing offensive attack, leading the league in team scoring by a wide margin. The Kings finished 42–31–7, good for second place in their division. That was a 23-point jump in the standings over the previous year. Gretzky broke team records for assists and points—and won his ninth Hart Trophy.

L.A. HERO

It all led up to a playoff confrontation worthy of a Hollywood scriptwriter—Wayne Gretzky and the Los Angeles Kings against the Edmonton Oilers.

Different uniform, same result—Gretzky celebrates after scoring a goal.

His old friends on the Oilers were now his opponents, and they didn't let up one bit on Gretzky. The Oilers jumped out to a three games to one lead in the series and the Kings looked finished. But the Kings won the next three games to take the series, sending southern California into a hockey-mad frenzy. It was a sweet victory for Gretzky, coming as it did against the team that had traded him away months earlier. The Kings lost their next series against Calgary, ending their season. But the team and its new star had come far.

For one thing, Gretzky was continuing to add to his career point total. By the end of his first season in Los Angeles, he was 13 points behind the record of 1,350 held by his boyhood idol, Gordie Howe. Clearly, Gretzky was about to shatter the record, but when? During the off-season, he looked over the 1989–90 schedule and figured that he could probably score 14 points by the sixth game of the season. The Kings' sixth game was in Edmonton, against the Oilers. It appeared Gretzky would have a chance at another big moment in the same city where he'd won four championships.

Sure enough, when the Kings traveled to Edmonton on October 15, Gretzky was just one point shy of tying the record. But it wasn't just doing it in Edmonton that gave Gretzky mixed feelings. He felt odd even breaking the record at all. Howe had always been a role model for Gretzky. Meeting him as a boy was a thrill. Playing against him in the old WHA was an even bigger thrill. Now Gretzky was aiming to erase Howe's name from the record books and replace it with his own. "It was the one record I wasn't sure I wanted to break," he remembered. "He's the best player ever and a part of me felt he should be remembered as having the most points ever."

But breaking the record was inevitable, as long as Gretzky kept playing hockey. In Edmonton, he shut himself in his hotel room until game time to avoid the crush of attention. Then, early in the game, he got an assist to tie the record. But the Oilers held him scoreless for most of the rest of the game. His old teammate Jeff Beukeboom even knocked him dizzy with a hard body check. As the clock wound down, the Edmonton fans began chanting Gretzky's name as if he'd never left. With about a minute left, Gretzky skated in front of the Oilers' net, where a loose puck bounced across the ice. Gretzky backhanded it into the goal. It was the backhand shot that Howe had told the 11-year-old Gretzky to practice years earlier. It made Gretzky the NHL's leading scorer.

Howe followed Gretzky from arena to arena so he could be sure to be in attendance when the record was broken. He cheered for Gretzky every step of the way. "The record didn't mean much to me until Wayne began to close in on it. Now it

With Mark Messier skating by, Gretzky jumps with joy after scoring his 1,851st point and breaking the NHL all-time scoring record.

means a lot," Howe said. "It's a true honor to have my record broken by a man like Wayne Gretzky. . . . I couldn't be prouder."

Howe was in Edmonton for the history-making game, as were Walter Gretzky and Janet Jones. They all joined Gretzky on the ice for a presentation ceremony. The league presented Gretzky with a silver tea tray. Even Mark Messier and the Oilers gave Gretzky a gold bracelet. But maybe the greatest gift was from Gordie Howe, who hugged Gretzky and told him, "Congratulations." The most remarkable thing about Gretzky's new record was how quickly he set it. Howe was fifty-one years old when he scored his last points. Gretzky was able to surpass his point total

Gretzky shakes hands with Gordie Howe while wife, Janet, and father, Walter, look on.

when he was still just twenty-eight. When Howe congratulated Gretzky on the ice in Edmonton that night, he inducted Gretzky into the ranks of sports' all-time greats. Now there were legions of hockey fans who idolized Gretzky the way he once idolized Howe.

Gretzky, of course, was far from finished, even if he was hockey's highest scorer. There were many accomplishments still to come. He led the once-lowly Kings to the Stanley Cup finals in 1993, setting off another wave of hockey mania in southern California. The Kings lost to the Canadiens that year, but Gretzky had an amazing play-off run, scoring 15 goals and 40 points in 24 games. It was a remarkable finish to a season that had seen him miss 39 games with injuries. The next year, he took another career record away from Gordie Howe, scoring his 802nd career goal to become the all-time NHL leader in that category.

SPOKESMAN FOR HOCKEY

But his greatest accomplishment in Los Angeles may well have been simply raising hockey's profile there. When he arrived in 1988, hockey was a curiosity in California, not a game that many people felt passionate about. Some had doubts that the sport could thrive in warm-weather cities like Los Angeles. Gretzky proved it could. In so doing,

*Gretzky grins and holds the puck he scored
his 802nd goal with.*

he helped change the face of the National Hockey League itself. Without Gretzky's leadership, hockey's leap to national popularity would not have been possible.

"I think people in the league were waiting to see what happened in L.A.," McNall says. "When they saw we were doing very well financially, they realized that putting more teams in California would be a natural. Obviously, Wayne's impact has been enormous. I knew his coming here would have a huge impact on the star, but I honestly didn't believe it was going to be as big as it has become. Certainly, it turned into more than a simple hockey trade."

With Gretzky making new fans for hockey wherever he went, the league expanded. Teams sprouted up in places that had never been considered hockey hotbeds. When Wayne Gretzky first started playing hockey, the game had been very popular only in Canada and a handful of northern American cities. Now, thanks to his achievements in the bright lights of Los Angeles, the game was becoming more American and even global.

In 1994 and 1995, the NHL suspended play during a dispute between players and owners. Never one to remain off the ice for very long, Gretzky organized an all-star squad of NHL stars for a European tour. The team was named the Ninety-Nines. For European fans, it meant a rare chance to see hockey's greatest player and other NHL stars up close. It's hard to imagine another player in any sport influential and popular enough to gather the best players in the world for an international exhibition tour. Gretzky had become hockey's ambassador to the world.

CHAPTER TEN

MOVING ON

Gretzky had spent ten glorious seasons in Edmonton and most of eight high-impact years in Los Angeles. But his four-month stint with the St. Louis Blues in 1996 was one of the lowest points in Gretzky's career.

Late in his eighth season with the Kings, Gretzky felt that the team was going nowhere and he asked to be traded. The Kings were no longer a playoff contender, and his friend Bruce McNall had sold the team. Gretzky was not used to sitting out the postseason on the sidelines and he didn't like it. He asked the Kings' management to either commit to building a winning team or trade him to a contender.

GRETZKY GETS THE BLUES

So on February 27, 1996, Gretzky was dealt to the Blues in exchange for three young players—Craig

Johnson, Patrice Tardiff, and Roman Vopat—and two draft picks. The deal promised to be a blockbuster. Gretzky would be playing for coach Mike Keenan, who had directed Gretzky to two Canada Cup championships. He'd be playing in the city where his wife, Janet Jones, grew up. And, best of all, he'd be paired with superstar winger Brett Hull. The president of the Blues said the trade was like "bringing in Mickey Mantle to play with Roger Maris."

No one was more excited about the trade than Hull. Just sharing the team bus with Gretzky seemed incredible to him. "I thought back to all the bus rides I took where I was sitting in the back of the bus saying, 'I wish we could have someone like Wayne Gretzky,'" Hull said. "Today, I thought that and I looked over and he's right there. I can't believe it." The Blues even made Gretzky team captain.

St. Louis fans couldn't believe it, either. At Gretzky's debut game in a St. Louis home uniform, they gave a long, deafening ovation that moved Gretzky visibly.

But things quickly turned sour in St. Louis. Again hampered by injury, Gretzky struggled. He and Hull never clicked. In the playoffs, things went so badly that Keenan even criticized Gretzky publicly, questioning his effort. Gretzky appeared to be moving slowly and gingerly, but he refused to use injuries as an excuse. "If he's not

Gretzky joined Brett Hull (left) on the St. Louis Blues. Unfortunately, the two players did not play well together and Gretzky soon left the team.

injured, something must be bothering him," Keenan told reporters after one game.

After the Blues were eliminated in the second round by the Detroit Red Wings, Gretzky flew home to Los Angeles. He and Jones had been searching for a permanent home in St. Louis, but after four miserable months with the Blues, they stopped looking. It was clear that Gretzky had seen enough of Mike Keenan and the Blues.

Gretzky was now a free agent for the first time in his career, able to sign with whatever team made him the best offer. On July 21, 1996, he signed a two-year, $8-million contract with the New York Rangers. Gretzky was ready to make a fresh start in the nation's biggest city.

NEW YORK, NEW YORK!

For Gretzky, joining the Rangers meant reuniting with his old friend from the Oilers, Mark Messier, who had led the Rangers to a Stanley Cup championship in 1994. But the Rangers were unable to duplicate the magic of that 1994 season and Messier soon left the Rangers for Vancouver. Gretzky posted solid numbers for the Rangers, but certainly not the spectacular statistics of his glory years. He finished the 1997 season with 97 points in 82 games.

Gretzky, Jones, and their three children moved into a penthouse apartment in Manhattan and settled into life in the big city. Gretzky was one of the sports world's biggest stars, living in the media capital of the world, and married to another celebrity. But he was determined to cre-

By joining the New York Rangers, Gretzky played once again with his old friend Mark Messier, who welcomed him onto the team with open arms.

ate a stable family environment away from the spotlight. He tried to spend as much time as possible with his children, Paulina, Trevor, and Ty.

Gretzky wanted his children to experience the same kind of family closeness he knew as a boy growing up in Brantford. Both he and Jones come from strong, middle-class families, and they drew on that strength to build successful careers at an early age. Of course, Gretzky was so successful that it was difficult for him to give his family the kind of "normal" life he would have liked. Constant travel took him away from home, and his every move drew the interest of fans and reporters. Then there was the pressure some people put on the children, to see if they could match the achievements of their father.

Their children showed an interest in hockey, participating in after-school skating groups and even making their own miniature cardboard rinks at home. Gretzky encouraged their interest in sports but was careful not to push them into activities that didn't interest them. "For Ty, I think there's so much pressure to play hockey, people watching him and seeing how good he is," Gretzky told a New York newspaper. "I've kind of stepped back and waited for them [the children] to come along."

Walter Gretzky had taken a similar approach with his sons decades earlier. No one played more

*Janet takes her two children for a walk in
Los Angeles. Gretzky was determined to give
his family a normal life.*

hockey or worked harder at the game as a boy than Wayne Gretzky—but always because he loved to play, not because he was forced to.

"Nowadays, people come up to me, dragging their kids behind them, and say, 'Wayne, tell my son to practice three hours a day like you did,'" Gretzky writes in his autobiography. "And I always say, 'I'm not going to tell him to practice three hours a day. Let him ride his bike if he wants.' Nobody told me to practice three hours a day. I practiced all day because I loved it. . . . The only way a kid is going to practice is if it's total fun for him—and it was for me."

His father helped make it fun for Gretzky. Walter Gretzky was always there, driving Wayne to practice, working with him on his skills in the backyard rink, sacrificing for him. It's a model Gretzky keeps in mind while raising his own family.

"Obviously, I'll never be the kind of father to my kids that my father was to me. It's a different lifestyle. My father never went out," Gretzky told a reporter. "He refused to go anywhere other than with his kids to hockey practices or with my sister wherever she went. For us, it's different. . . . We have to travel, so when we are home, we try to make life as normal as possible. . . . We are loving to our kids, we're affectionate to them and that's what it's all about."

Wayne and his father share a laugh early in his career. The two never forgot that hockey was a game to be enjoyed.

Even after Wayne Gretzky became famous and made millions, his father kept his service job with Bell Canada. He declined his son's offers of a new house and new cars. Walter and Phyllis Gretzky still live in the house on Varadi Avenue where they raised their family.

When a brain aneurysm threatened his father's life in 1991, Gretzky feared that he would lose the man who had been his coach, agent, teacher, and role model. For several weeks, the elder Gretzky was critically ill. Afterward, he suffered from memory loss. He could not recall many of his son's great moments on ice and worse, he had trouble recognizing his grandchildren. Eventually, Walter Gretzky recovered enough to coach youth hockey in Brantford.

Wayne Gretzky, leading a superstar's life in the big city, has not forgotten that he owes much of his success to his father, his family, and his upbringing in Brantford.

CHAPTER ELEVEN

GRETZKY AND THE GLOBAL GAME

Wayne Gretzky may have been still a teenager when he broke into the National Hockey League in 1979, and he was extraordinarily talented, but he had one thing in common with most of the other players—he was Canadian. For the entire history of the sport, Canadians had dominated the game. They developed it, made it their national pastime, and produced the best players. Hockey was played professionally in the United States, but the U.S. teams were stocked mostly with Canadian players.

HOCKEY GOES GLOBAL

During the course of Gretzky's long career, however, something began to change. More Americans took to the sport, both as spectators and players. And the game took root not only in cold-weather cities, but also in the southern states of the Sun Belt, where ice was once seen only in soft drinks. Young hockey players took to the game with a passion—and when they couldn't find ice, they played on asphalt with in-line skates. Americans, such as Chris Chelios and Keith Tkachuk, established themselves as stars in the NHL.

More and more European players made their mark in the NHL, too. Jaromir Jagr and Dominik Hasek came from the Czech Republic, Jari Kurri from Finland, and Peter Forsberg from Sweden. In just two decades, the makeup of the NHL changed from almost entirely Canadian to a diverse array of nationalities. Canada's game had become the world's game. By 1998, 61 percent of NHL players were Canadian, 16 percent were American, and 6 percent were Russian. Players from Sweden and the Czech Republic accounted for about 5 percent each. Many of them had grown up watching Gretzky work his magic for the Edmonton Oilers and Los Angeles Kings. There was no better evidence of this change than two international events within a month of each other in 1998—the NHL All-Star Game and the Winter Olympics.

The All-Star Game in Vancouver was the first to match North American stars against stars from the rest of the world. It was also Gretzky's seventeenth consecutive All-Star appearance—a record.

His two assists in North America's 8–7 victory made him the leading scorer in All-Star history. But European stars showed their firepower, too, scoring three goals on their first five shots. Two were by Finland's Teemu Selanne, who won the game's Most Valuable Player award.

Just a month later came an even clearer demonstration of the change in the balance of hockey power. At the Winter Olympics in Nagano, Japan, the favored Canadian team lost to the Czech Republic, who went on to win the gold medal. It was the first time professional hockey players had competed in the Olympics. For Wayne Gretzky and the rest of the Canadian team, it was a chance to regain Canada's dominance after some disappointing performances in international play. Gretzky had always come up big representing his country in international play, but even he couldn't rescue the Canadians. The Czech team, behind Dominik Hasek's incredible goaltending, was not to be denied.

It was a bitter disappointment for Gretzky. After so many achievements in his career, this was his first shot at an Olympic gold medal and, at age 37, he knew it was probably also his last. When the Canadian team was eliminated, and his hopes for Olympic gold dashed, Gretzky was near tears.

Nevertheless, the Olympic tournament was a tribute to how popular worldwide hockey had

Discouraged, Gretzky leaves the ice after Canada was defeated in the 1998 Olympics.

become in the Gretzky era. It was also a tribute to the magnitude of Gretzky's stardom. At the Olympic Village in Nagano, he turned the heads of even other star athletes. He was the most recognizable athlete at the games, and he attracted attention everywhere he went. Typically, Gretzky remained down to earth amid all the hype. He had the same basic living quarters as all the other athletes, and even waited his turn to use the shared bathroom. He tried to blend in with his teammates and demanded no special treatment. The Olympics may have ended in disappointment for Gretzky, but the world saw the class that makes him one of our most idolized athletes.

SKILL AND CLASS

It is all too rare for public figures to be both highly successful and very popular. Sometimes, the higher a star climbs, the more people resent the person. But Gretzky is different. He's the greatest player ever to lace up skates, and virtually everyone in the hockey world has wonderful things to say about him. It might be because Gretzky's kind of greatness reflects well on those around him. His passing skills mean more points for players skating with him, his team leadership means more wins, and his hard work and dedication make him a role model for other players. Even off

Even under the crushing attention of the press, Gretzky has always remained calm and patient.

the ice, Gretzky is remarkably selfless, patiently answering reporters' questions, treating teammates and opponents with respect, and taking the time to talk to and help the less fortunate. "Thank God he is the person he is," said Colleen Howe, the wife of Gordie Howe. "Because Wayne is bigger than the league."

Asked to rate Gretzky on a scale from one to ten, hockey great Phil Esposito answered, "He's a sixty." Esposito was one of the stars whose records Gretzky shattered on his march through NHL history. As Esposito's comment suggests, it is almost impossible to measure Gretzky's impact on hockey. Conventional statistics don't really do his performance justice.

Like baseball's Babe Ruth, Gretzky's impact on the game he played was so strong that it changed the way the game was played. When Gretzky made his debut in the National Hockey League, the sport was dominated by teams that emphasized bruising body checks and rough play. Gretzky reminded the hockey world that there was room for finesse and intelligence. He helped reintroduce passing skills to the game. His creativity and grace on the ice proved to be just as important as size or speed.

Of course, Gretzky didn't just shape how the game was played, but where it was played. His popularity brought an era of NHL expansion that has firmly entrenched hockey in the Sun Belt.

Then there are Gretzky's career marks. He is the NHL's leading career goal scorer; the career leader in points; the career leader in assists; nine times the NHL's Most Valuable Player; and holder of no less than 61 NHL records.

*Today, Gretzky continues to play hockey with
the passion and skill that has made him
"The Great One."*

Gretzky's long list of records and championships is phenomenal—his honors and victories rank him as the most dominant athlete in any sport in recent times. They're even more impressive when you consider that he did it all while winning friends and admirers everywhere he went.

In so many ways, Wayne Gretzky is the best thing that ever happened to hockey.

1961	Born on January 26 in Brantford, Ontario
1967	Begins playing novice hockey
1972	Scores 378 goals in 69 novice games, earning his nickname "The Great Gretzky"
	Meets Gordie Howe
1975	Begins playing Junior B hockey in Toronto
1977	Begins wearing number 99
1978	Wins Ontario Hockey Association Rookie of the Year honors
	Signs contract with Indianapolis Racers of the World Hockey Association
1979	Traded to Edmonton Oilers
1980	Wins first of nine Hart Trophies as NHL's Most Valuable Player
1981	Scores 50 goals in first 39 games

1984	Leads Oilers to Stanley Cup victory
1988	Marries Janet Jones
	Traded to Los Angeles Kings
1989	Becomes NHL's all-time points leader, breaking Gordie Howe's record
1993	Leads Kings to Stanley Cup finals
1994	Becomes NHL's all-time leading goal-scorer
1996	Traded to St. Louis Blues
	Signs with New York Rangers
1998	Plays in Winter Olympics in Nagano, Japan

Gretzky: An Autobiography (New York: Harper-Collins, 1990) by Gretzky with Rick Reilly is a comprehensive and readable chronicle of the player's life and career. The chapters on Gretzky's early years as a hockey prodigy are especially strong. Gretzky collaborated on another, earlier autobiography, *Gretzky: From Backyard Rink to the Stanley Cup* (New York: Avon Books, 1984).

Gretzky has been the subject of numerous biographies, most notably *The Great Gretzky* by Stan Fischler (New York: Quill, 1982). *Wayne Gretzky* (New York: House of Collectibles, 1996) is part of the Beckett Great Sports Heroes series. Collectors of sports memorabilia will find its sections on Gretzky collectibles valuable, and very young readers may like the Gretzky comic that is included.

The Official National Hockey League 75th Anniversary Commemorative Book (Toronto: McClelland and Stewart, 1991) offers an excellent history of the NHL and a useful chapter on Gretzky's impact on the game.

FOR FURTHER READING

BOOKS:

Duplacey, James. *The Annotated Rules of Hockey*. New York: Lyons & Burford, 1996.

Esposito, Phil. *Hockey Is My Life*. New York: Dodd, Mead, 1972.

Fischler, Stan. *The Great Gretzky*. New York: Quill, 1982.

Gretzky, Wayne, with Rick Reilly. *Gretzky: An Autobiography*. New York: HarperCollins, 1990.

Gretzky, Wayne, and Jim Taylor. *Gretzky: From Backyard Rink to the Stanley Cup*. New York: Avon Books, 1984

MacSkimming, Roy. *Gordie: A Hockey Legend*. Vancouver: Greystone Books, 1994.

The Official National Hockey League 75th Anniversary Commemorative Book. Toronto: McClelland and Stewart, 1991.

Wayne Gretzky. New York: House of Collectibles, 1996.

INTERNET RESOURCES:

Because of the changeable nature of the Internet, sites appear and disappear very quickly. These resources offered useful information on Wayne Gretzky at the time of publication. Internet addresses must be entered with capital and lowercase letters exactly as they appear.

http://www.gretzky.com
This site offers the latest statistics and game results, as well as biographical information and video and audio clips from Gretzky's career.

http://www.puckplace.com
Along with news and information on Gretzky, this site provides links to other hockey-related sites.

http://www.nhl.com
This site is the official home page of the National Hockey League (NHL). It contains stories about the league and links to all NHL teams.

INDEX

Page numbers in *italics* indicate illustrations.

Anderson, Glenn, 41, 52

Bailey, Ace, 38
Beliveau, Jean, 22, 52
Beukeboom, Jeff, 77
Boston Bruins, 63
Brantford, Ontario, 10, 13, 14, 22, 23, 30, 89, 93
Brantford Atom League, 14
Brantford Nadrofsky novice team, 14–16, 18
Bumbacco, Angelo, 24, 25

Canada Cup series, 46–47, 60, 64–65, 66, 85
Carson, Jimmy, 65
Chelios, Chris, 95
Clarke, Bobby, 41
Coffey, Paul, 41
Costner, Kevin, 71

Detroit Red Wings, 87
Dionne, Marcel, 39

Edmonton Oilers, 31–57, 63–68, 73, 74–76, 78–79, 84, 87, 95
Esposito, Phil, 26, 41, 47, 100

Fogolin, Lee, 52
Forsberg, Peter, 95

Gelinas, Martin, 65
Gretzky, Brent (brother), 14, 23, 47, *56*, 57
Gretzky, Glen (brother), 14
Gretzky, Keith (brother), 14
Gretzky, Kim (sister), 13, 14, 91
Gretzky, Paulina (daughter), 87, 89
Gretzky, Phyllis (mother), 13, 23, 47, 48, 93

Gretzky, Trevor (son), 87, 89
Gretzky, Ty (son), 87, 89
Gretzky, Walter (father), 9–11, *12*, 13, 17, 23, 38, 47, 48, 49–50, 78, 89–93, *92*
Gretzky, Wayne
  autobiography, 13, 16, 91
  awards, 17, 35, 39–40, 44, 51, 74, 100
  birth, 13
  and Canada Cup series, 46–47, 60, 64–65, 66, 85
  childhood, 9–27, 89
  early hockey career, 14–22, *19*, 21
  as Edmonton Oiler, 31–57, *32, 34, 37, 40, 42, 46, 49, 53, 55, 56*, 63–68, *64, 67, 69*, 84, 87, 95
  education, 18, 23, 25
  and his family, 13–14, 23, 87–93, *92*
  "greatness" of, 18, 98–102, *99*
  as Indianapolis Racer, 28–31
  in international competitions, 46–47, 60, 64–65, 82–83, 96–98, *97*
  as Los Angeles King, 28–30, 65–84, *69, 70, 72, 75*, 95
  marriage, 58–62, *61*
  minor league career, 22–27

  joins NHL, 28–30, 94
  as New York Ranger, *15*, 87, *88, 101*
  and 1998 All-Star Game, 95–96
  and 1998 Winter Olympics, 95, 96–98, *97*
  and Ninety-Nines, 82–83
  in playoffs, 33–35, 40–44, 48–50, 54, 63, 66, 74–76, 80, 85
  records, 18, 41, 45–48, 51, 52, 74, 76–80, *78, 79, 81*, 95, 100, 102
  as Saint Louis Blue, 84–87, *86*
  wins Stanley Cup, 54–57, *55, 56*, 63, *64*, 65, *68*
  in WHA, 27, 28–35, *29, 32, 34*, 65, 77

Hartford Whalers, 36. *See also* New England Whalers
Hart Trophy, 39–40, 44, 51, 63, 74, 100
Hasek, Dominik, 95, 96
"Hockey Night in Canada," 13, 52
Hodge, Ken, 26
Howe, Colleen, 99
Howe, Gordy, 22, 26, 27, 30, 51, 76–78, 79–80, *79*, 99
Hull, Bobby, 27
Hull, Brett, 85, *86*

Indianapolis Racers, 28–31

Jagr, Jaromir, 95
Johnson, Craig, 84–85
Jones, Janet (wife), 58–62, *59, 61,* 66, 68, 78, 85, 87, 88, *90*
Junior Hockey, 11, 22–27

Keenan, Mike, 85–87
Krushelnyski, Mike, 65
Kurri, Jari, 41, 52

Lady Byng Trophy, 39
Lafleur, Guy, 39
Lemieux, Mario, 65
Los Angeles Kings, 28–30, 48, 65–84, 95
Lowe, Kevin, 37–38

McNall, Bruce, 68, *70,* 82, 84
MacPherson, Muzz, 24–25, 26
McSorley, Marty, 65
Messier, Mark, 37–38, *64,* 78, *78,* 87, *88*
Montreal Canadiens, 22, 41–43, 80
Moog, Andy, 41

National Hockey League (NHL), 26, 31, 33, 35, 36–57, 63–87, 100
    expansion of, 36, 71, 82, 94–96
New England Whalers, 30. *See also* Hartford Whalers

New York Islanders, 44, 49, 54
New York Rangers, 44, 87
Ninety-Nines, 82–83

Ontario Hockey Association (OHA), 25
Orr, Bobby, 41, 52

Philadelphia Flyers, 40–41, 47
Pittsburgh Penguins, 65
Pocklington, Peter, 33, 65, 66

Quebec Nordiques, 36

Saint Louis Blues, 84–87
Sather, Glen, 31–33, 38, 66
Sault Ste. Marie Greyhounds, 24–26, 44
Selanne, Teemu, 96
Skalbania, Nelson, 28, 31
Stallone, Sylvester, 71
Stanley Cup, 48, 50, 51–52, 54–57, 63, 65, 68
Stefan, Greg, 20

Tardiff, Patrice, 85
Tkachuk, Keith, 95

Vopat, Roman, 85

Wally Coliseum, 10–11, 14
Winnipeg Jets, 33, 36
World Hockey Association (WHA), 27–36, 41, 65, 77

ABOUT THE AUTHOR

Andrew Santella lives in Chicago. He writes about sports and other topics for magazines ranging from *Details* to *Nickelodeon* to *Chicago*. He has interviewed such sports greats as Randy Johnson, Jeff Gordon, Ozzie Smith, and Benny the Bull. He is the author of several Children's Press titles, including *Jackie Robinson Breaks the Color Line* and *Chisholm Trail*.